50

LISTS FOR
FEMINISTS

ABRAMS NOTERIE, NEW YORK

LIST YOUR POLITICAL ISSUES

What are your priorities when you head to the polls?

_____

_____

_____

_____

_____

_____

_____

_____

* Suffragist, abolitionist, and activist Susan B. Anthony (1820–1906)
traveled around the country advocating for women's rights, and she
worked hard her whole life to pass the suffrage amendment. She met
and befriended Senator Aaron Sargent on a train ride in 1872.

THE NINETEENTH AMENDMENT:
The Susan B. Anthony* Amendment

American suffragists lobbied, marched, lectured, and fought for decades to gain the basic civil right to vote. The Nineteenth Amendment was first introduced by Senator Aaron A. Sargent in 1878, but it took until World War I for Congress to submit it for ratification. In 1918, President Woodrow Wilson gave an impassioned speech to the Senate applauding women's efforts in the war and calling for equal suffrage. The amendment was finally ratified on August 18, 1920.

"The right of citizens of the United States to vote shall not be denied or abridged by the United States or by any state on account of sex."

THE NINETEENTH AMENDMENT

SADIE TANNER MOSSELL ALEXANDER:
The First African American Woman to Earn a PhD

A woman of many firsts, Sadie Tanner Mossell Alexander (1898–1989) became the first black woman to earn a PhD in the United States (in economics in 1921), to graduate from the University of Pennsylvania Law School (in 1927), and to be admitted to the Pennsylvania Bar. A distinguished lawyer, Alexander also served President Harry S. Truman's administration as a member of the President's Committee on Civil Rights in 1947. This committee ultimately led Truman to call for a federal law outlawing lynching.

LIST THE TRAILBLAZERS IN YOUR LIFE

Who has shown you what is possible, by their own example?

"I never looked for anybody to hold the door open for me. I knew well that the only way I could get that door open was to knock it down; because I knocked all of them down."

SADIE TANNER MOSSELL ALEXANDER

LIST YOUR CAUSES

What foundations, nonprofits, or other programs do you support?

_____

_____

_____

_____

_____

_____

_____

"No woman can call herself free who does not own and control her body."

MARGARET SANGER

MARGARET SANGER AND THE AMERICAN BIRTH CONTROL LEAGUE

Sex educator, writer, and nurse Margaret Sanger (1879–1966) founded the American Birth Control League (ABCL) in 1921 and opened its first legal clinic in 1923. The ABCL conducted research on contraception, educated and encouraged women to control their own fertility, and fought for legislative support by organizing conferences and publishing a monthly journal. These efforts helped to disseminate accurate information about contraceptives. In 1942, the ABCL became the Planned Parenthood Federation of America, which is still active today.

LIST YOUR PERSONAL LIBERTIES

What social norms do you eschew?

_____

_____

_____

_____

_____

_____

_____

THE FLAPPERS: The Party Women of the Jazz Age

In 1922, _The Flapper_* published its first issue, proudly introducing a fashionable woman who breaks with traditional values to embrace freedom and modernity. Notably, the "flapper" rejected wearing a corset, empowering her to become more active in social life outside the home. Though many found flappers outrageous and downright threatening to conventional society, some now consider them the first generation of independent American women—women who pushed social, political, and sexual barriers.

Bobbed hair

Straight, loose-fitting clothes

No corset

Dropped waistline

Short skirt

High heels

The Flapper was a small magazine based out of Chicago. Its tagline was "Not for Old Fogies."

LIST YOUR INTELLECTUAL INTERESTS

What are you curious about?

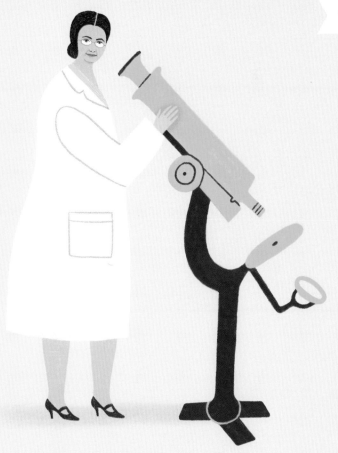

FLORENCE SABIN:
The First Lady of American Science

Florence Sabin (1871–1953) was the first woman to graduate from Johns Hopkins University Medical School, in 1900, and became its first female full professor in 1917. In 1925, she became the first female member of the National Academy of Sciences. A pioneering medical researcher, Sabin is best known for her research on brain structure, the lymphatic system, blood cells, and tuberculosis.

"I hope my studies may be an encouragement to other women, especially to young women, to devote their lives to the larger interests of the mind."

FLORENCE SABIN

GERTRUDE CAROLINE EDERLE:
Queen of the Waves

Olympic gold medalist Gertrude Caroline Ederle (1905–2003) made history in 1926 by becoming the first woman to swim the English Channel. Despite tricky currents, Ederle swam the 35-mile stretch from France to England in 14 hours 31 minutes, breaking the men's world record by 1 hour 59 minutes! Her achievement won her fame and the nicknames "Queen of the Waves" and "America's best girl." Ederle's hearing was irreversibly damaged by the swim, but her disability inspired her to become a swimming instructor for deaf children.

England

LIST YOUR CRAZIEST GOALS

What's your version of swimming the English Channel?

_____

_____

_____

_____

_____

_____

France

LIST YOUR STYLE ICONS

Who are your "It Girls," your influencers, the bold ones who always seem to be pointing toward the future?

CLARA BOW:
The Original "It Girl"

In 1928, movie star Clara Gordon Bow (1905–1965), nicknamed the "It* Girl," was featured on the cover of *Vanity Fair* gleefully wearing a bathing suit that exposed her shoulders and legs. To many, this cover was utterly scandalous and indecent. Yet other young women happily followed her example: shorter skirts, smaller bathing suits, more bare skin. Bow's bold pose and even bolder garment perfectly encapsulate the audacity and newfound freedom that many women felt in the 1920s.

* The nickname came from her performance in the film *It*, a silent romantic comedy from 1927.

LIST YOUR ACTS OF GOOD

How do you give back to your community?

_____

_____

_____

_____

_____

_____

_____

_____

_____

_____

JANE ADDAMS:
The First American Woman to Receive the Nobel Peace Prize

Known as "the mother of social work," Jane Addams (1860–1935) founded Hull-House in 1889, with her friend Ellen G. Starr (1859–1940), which provided social services to the immigrant and poor population living in the Chicago area. A public advocate for peace, Addams was appointed chair of the Women's Peace Party in 1915 and later served as president of the International Congress of Women at The Hague. In 1931 she became the first American woman to be awarded the Nobel Peace Prize.

LIST YOUR ACTS OF BRAVERY, BIG OR SMALL

When have you taken a flier?

_____

_____

_____

_____

_____

_____

AMELIA EARHART: Queen of the Air

In 1932, Amelia Earhart (1897–c. 1939) became the first woman to fly alone over the Atlantic Ocean, flying from Newfoundland, Canada, to Culmore, Northern Ireland. This amazing achievement earned her the Distinguished Flying Cross and opened new frontiers for women. Earhart was also a member of the National Woman's Party and a supporter of equal rights for women. In 1937, while attempting to fly around the globe, she mysteriously disappeared over the Pacific Ocean, but she is remembered for her bravery and extraordinary triumphs, both in aviation and for women.

ELEANOR ROOSEVELT: A New Kind of First Lady

Eleanor Roosevelt (1884–1962) became First Lady in 1933, a position she dramatically redefined over twelve years in the role. Not content hosting dinners, Roosevelt was active in the public eye, working avidly for human rights, children's causes, and women's issues. She encouraged major publications to employ women—in fact, only female reporters could gain access to her press conferences. An independent spirit, Roosevelt had her own daily syndicated newspaper column for twenty-seven years, called "My Day," in which she reflected upon her life.

"Do what you
feel in your heart
to be right."

ELEANOR ROOSEVELT

LIST YOUR DAILY ROUTINE

What does your everyday schedule look like?

_____

_____

_____

_____

_____

_____

_____

_____

_____

_____

WOMEN AND WORLD WAR II

During World War II, when men joined the military in droves, more than six million women entered the workforce. Many worked positions previously closed to women, such as office and factory jobs. The greatest increase in female workers was in manufacturing: More than 2.5 million women joined factories during the war. In 1942, Congress established women's branches in each of the armed services, and approximately 350,000 women joined the military during the war, replacing men in many noncombat jobs like truck driving, engineering, and clerical work.

LIST YOUR BIGGEST LIFE OBSTACLES

What have you done to overcome them?

LIST YOUR PASSION PROJECTS

When you have downtime, where do you spend your energy?

_____

_____

_____

_____

_____

_____

_____

LIST YOUR HAPPY PLACES

Where do you go for peace of mind?

_____

_____

_____

_____

_____

_____

_____

WONDER WOMAN: Goddess of Love and War

A superhero. A goddess. A feminist icon. Introduced during World War II, Wonder Woman uses her superhuman strength and speed, bullet-proof bracelets and awesome golden Lasso of Truth to fight evil while bringing a message of peace and love to the world. Inspired by burgeoning feminism and the writings of Margaret Sanger, Wonder Woman was the brainchild of psychologist and writer William Moulton Marston, who set out to create a powerful heroine who embodied feminist ideals.

LIST YOUR SUPERHEROES, REAL OR FICTIONAL

Who should rule the world?

_____

_____

_____

_____

_____

_____

_____

"Frankly, Wonder Woman is psychological propaganda for the new type of woman who, I believe, should rule the world."

WILLIAM MOULTON MARSTON

THE LANGLEY "COMPUTERS"

The push for aeronautical advancement grew during World War II, and in 1935 women were brought into the Langley Memorial Aeronautical Laboratory to do calculations by hand in order to free up the (white, male) engineers for other work. These women "computers" went largely unnoticed by the public, especially the African American computers, who were not hired at Langley until the 1940s. These mathematicians greatly contributed to the development of wartime aircrafts, making them faster and safer, and later to the space race during the Cold War.

LIST YOUR NOT-SO-HIDDEN TALENTS

What do you excel at?

LIST YOUR MEDIA INFLUENCES

What did you read or listen to growing up?

_____

_____

_____

_____

_____

What about now?

_____

_____

_____

_____

_____

SEVENTEEN MAGAZINE

The quintessential magazine for teenage girls, *Seventeen* recognized the rising power of teenagers and emerging youth culture by dedicating itself to the new demographic group. One of the magazine's original goals was to provide teenage girls with role models of working women and to introduce them to different career paths, while also discussing fashion, leisure activities, politics, and social issues relevant to teens. It even included fiction—Sylvia Plath had a story published there in 1950.

> "*Seventeen* is your magazine, High School Girls of America—all yours! . . . You're going to have to run this show—so the sooner you start thinking about it, the better."
>
> HELEN VALENTINE,
> FIRST EDITOR IN CHIEF
> OF *SEVENTEEN*

LIST YOUR AWARDS

Jot down any prizes, accolades, or achievements that you're proud of.

"I think I opened the gate for [future black track stars]. Whether they think that or not, they should be grateful to someone in the black race who was able to do these things."

ALICE MARIE COACHMAN

ALICE MARIE COACHMAN:
First Black Female Olympic Gold Medalist

In 1948, Alice Marie Coachman (1923–2014) became the first black woman ever to win an Olympic gold medal. Specializing in the high jump, Coachman leaped 5 feet 6 ⅛ inches (1.68 meters) on her first try in the high jump finals. She was the only American woman to win gold in the 1948 London Olympics. Coachman was inducted into the United States Olympic Hall of Fame in 2004 and received recognition for paving the way for future African American track stars.

THE HAZEL SCOTT SHOW

Hazel Scott (1920–1981) was a jazz musician extraordinaire. Born in Trinidad, she moved to New York City at the age of four. As a child, Scott was a musical prodigy, and she grew up to become a dynamic and bold performer. She performed on radio and television programs, in nightclubs, on Broadway, and in films. Scott was also a pioneer: On July 3, 1950, she became the first black person to host her own TV show, *The Hazel Scott Show,* which showcased her range as a performer and musician. Later in her career, Scott and her then husband, Adam Clayton Powell Jr., leveraged her fame to support the fight for racial equality and civil rights.

LIST YOUR CREATIVE PURSUITS

What hobbies and activities do you do to express yourself?

_____

_____

_____

_____

_____

_____

_____

_____

_____

LIST YOUR RESISTANCE

What moves can you make to challenge the status quo?

_____

_____

_____

_____

_____

_____

_____

_____

_____

_____

ROSA PARKS: First Lady of Civil Rights

Rosa Parks (1913–2005) was riding a Montgomery, Alabama, bus home on December 1, 1955, angry and deeply saddened by recent racist violence. When the driver asked her to relinquish her seat in the "colored section" to a white passenger, Parks, a respected civil rights activist, refused. She was arrested for civil disobedience, but her act of defiance sparked the Montgomery bus boycott, led by Martin Luther King Jr., and ignited the civil rights movement. The NAACP tapped Parks to fight for the cause in courts, and in late 1956, the Supreme Court ruled that Montgomery's segregated seating was unconstitutional.

LIST YOUR SUPPORT SYSTEMS

What circles can you lean on? Who are you, in turn, lifting up?

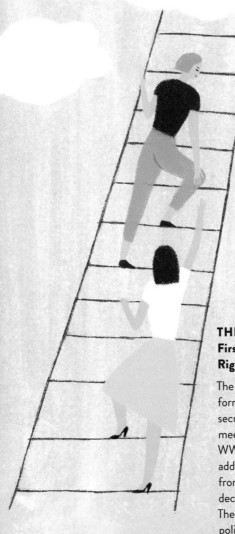

THE DAUGHTERS OF BILITIS:
First Lesbian Civil and Political Rights Organization

The Daughters of Bilitis* (DOB) was formed in San Francisco in 1955 as a secret social club where lesbians could meet and share their experiences. Post-WWII, the LGBTQAI+ community faced additional prejudice and discrimination from the State Department, which declared homosexuality a security threat. The DOB later developed into a more politically focused organization, with a mission to support and educate lesbian women. They released a newsletter titled *The Ladder*, the first nationally distributed lesbian magazine in the United States.

LIST YOUR CHILDHOOD PASTIMES

How did they contribute to who you are today?

_____

_____

_____

_____

_____

_____

_____

_____

_____

BARBIE: More Than a Doll

When the first Barbie doll was sold by Mattel in 1959, it was revolutionary. Women were expected to be full-time mothers and homemakers, and toys reflected this: The market consisted mostly of baby dolls. Barbie enabled girls to aspire to other careers through role-play, with Barbie portraying everything from astronauts and surgeons to reporters and rappers. Though controversial for her unrealistic body, Barbie is nevertheless a cultural icon that has shaped the imaginations of many generations of girls.

HELEN GURLEY BROWN'S
SEX AND THE SINGLE GIRL

In 1962, Helen Gurley Brown (1922–
2012), editor in chief of *Cosmopolitan* for
thirty-two years, published her book *Sex
and the Single Girl*. It was a scandalous
sensation and sold two million copies
in three weeks. Written as an advice
book, it covers topics such as career,
fashion, love, and entertainment. Most
important, it provocatively encourages
unmarried women to become financially
independent and experience sexual
relationships out of wedlock. The book
recognized the 1960s' newly prolonged
state of singlehood not only as legitimate,
but also as a time of life to celebrate.

"[Life is] a good
show . . . enjoy it from
wherever you are,
whether it's two in
the balcony or one on
the aisle–don't miss
any of it."

HELEN GURLEY BROWN

LIST YOUR SELF-CARE HABITS

How do you take care of yourself?
What keeps you strong and healthy?

_____

_____

_____

_____

_____

_____

_____

_____

_____

THE CIVIL RIGHTS ACT

On July 2, 1964, the Civil Rights Act was signed into law by President Lyndon B. Johnson. Notably, Title VII in the act prohibits labor discrimination on the basis of race, color, religion, sex, or national origin, and was a significant step toward ensuring equality in the workforce. The word "sex" was actually added to Title VII as an afterthought; opponents to the act hoped that the inclusion of gender equality would sound so preposterous that it would lead to the act's dismissal. Luckily, that was not the case.

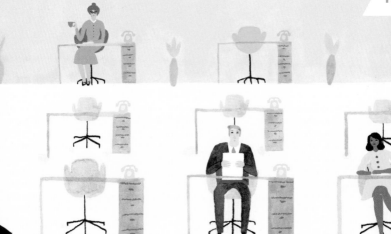

LIST YOUR CAREER ASPIRATIONS

What do you dream of doing with your work life?

_____

_____

_____

_____

_____

LIST YOUR FEARS

Rational or irrational, deep-seated or brand
new, write them all here and consider this
your first step toward conquering them.

_____

_____

_____

_____

_____

_____

THE FEMINIST PROTEST AT THE MISS AMERICA PAGEANT:
"All Women Are Beautiful!"

On September 7, 1968, on the boardwalk of Atlantic City, a feminist
demonstration rallied against the Miss America Pageant, which they considered
degrading to women, by giving the crown to a sheep and likening the pageant
to a cattle auction. Protesters also tossed feminine objects of oppression—bras,
hairspray, false eyelashes—into a "freedom trash can." Contrary to popular belief,
these objects were never burned, but the term "bra burners" was coined, and the
sensational event drew worldwide media attention to the feminist movement.

SHIRLEY CHISHOLM: "Unbossed and Unbought"

"Unbossed and unbought" was Shirley Chisholm's (1924–2005) motto. It reflected her bold and unapologetic championing of women and minorities. In 1968, she became the first black woman elected to the US Congress, where she represented New York for seven terms, from 1969 to 1983. Chisholm made sure that all her office staff members were women and that half were black. Chisholm said she didn't want to be remembered as "the first black woman congressman" but that she'd "like them to say that Shirley Chisholm had guts."*

"In the end anti-black, anti-female, and all forms of discrimination are equivalent to the same thing—anti-humanism."

SHIRLEY CHISHOLM

LIST YOUR FAVORITE QUOTES AND MOTTOS

What words of wisdom do you constantly turn to?

*In 1972, Chisholm became the first black candidate and woman to run for a major party's presidential nomination. As a woman, she received very little support from Democratic party members or from her black male colleagues, and there was no mainstream media coverage on her campaign.

THE REDSTOCKINGS: Sisterhood Is Powerful

A radical feminist group, known as the Redstockings,* was formed in New York City in early 1969. They believed patriarchal society was exploitative, destructive, and oppressive, and maintained that women are never to blame for their oppression. The group organized frequent speaking sessions to discuss how sexism influences women's lives. In March 1969, they famously protested a legislative hearing about prohibiting abortions by holding an abortion "speak-out." Today, the Redstockings exist as a grassroots think tank focused on women's liberation issues.

LIST YOUR POWERS

**Think about the kinds of things people ask of you—
what are you known for?**

_____

_____

_____

_____

_____

_____

_____

_____

*A play on "Bluestockings," a derogatory term for
feminists in the eighteenth and nineteenth centuries.

THE MARY TYLER MOORE SHOW:
"TV's first truly female-dominated sitcom"

The Mary Tyler Moore Show broke all the rules
of television. The highly acclaimed sitcom
aired on CBS from 1970 to 1977, with Mary
Tyler Moore starring as Mary Richards—a
single, independent, career-focused woman
who worked as a TV producer. The show
addressed bold feminist topics such as
equal pay for women, premarital sex, and
homosexuality. Portraying realistic and
complex characters, it paved the way for
women in television and empowered women
behind the scenes, too: By 1973, a third of
the shows' writers were women.

LIST YOUR SILVER OR BIG SCREEN HEROINES

Which TV or film characters inspire you?

BILLIE JEAN KING AND THE BATTLE OF THE SEXES

Former top-ranking tennis player and self-proclaimed chauvinist Bobby Riggs met his match in 1973, when he challenged Billie Jean King (b. 1943), then the world's number-one ranked female tennis player, to a televised game. The match set the record for the largest tennis audience and the largest prize awarded at the time—which went to King. The first prominent female athlete to come out as bisexual and to win the Presidential Medal of Freedom, King is an advocate for gender equality and helped found the Women's Tennis Association.

LIST YOUR BATTLES

Large or small, list some moments when you beat the odds.

_____

_____

_____

_____

_____

_____

_____

_____

_____

LIST YOUR INVESTMENTS

Personal, financial, or otherwise—
what are you investing in for the long term?

_____

_____

_____

_____

_____

_____

MONEY OF HER OWN: The Equal Credit Opportunity Act

Before 1974, many banks required single, widowed, or divorced women to bring a man to cosign any credit application, regardless of the woman's income. When the government's banking committee outlined the Equal Credit Opportunity Act, it focused on racial and social discrimination. Louisiana congresswoman Lindy Boggs (1916–2013) added the terms "sex" and "marital status", only informing other members after she distributed her version of the bill. The committee unanimously approved the act, which prohibited financial institutions from discriminating against applicants for credit on the basis of race, color, religion, national origin, sex, marital status, or age.

"Knowing the Members composing this committee as well as I do, I'm sure it was just an oversight that we didn't have 'sex' or 'marital status' included. I've taken care of that."

LINDY BOGGS

LIST YOUR OUTLETS

What do you do to blow off steam?

_____

_____

_____

_____

_____

LIST YOUR RESOLUTIONS

How would you like to turn over a new leaf?

_____

_____

_____

_____

_____

SALLY RIDE:
First American Woman in Space

A mission specialist on the *Challenger* space shuttle, Dr. Sally Ride (1951–2012) became the first American woman to go to space in 1983. During her history-making flight, Ride worked the robotic arm to help launch satellites into orbit. Ride cofounded the organization Sally Ride Science in 2001 to encourage women and girls to study science, mathematics, and technology. Ride was also the first acknowledged gay astronaut, though this was revealed only at the time of her death.

"I would like to be remembered as someone who was not afraid to do what she wanted to do, and as someone who took risks along the way in order to achieve her goals."

SALLY RIDE

LIST YOUR WILDEST TRAVEL ADVENTURES

Where have you been?

_____

_____

_____

_____

_____

Where will you go next?

_____

_____

_____

_____

_____

"I'm tough, I'm ambitious, and I know exactly what I want."

MADONNA

MADONNA: Queen of Pop

World-famous singer, songwriter, actress, and pop-culture icon Madonna (b. 1958) released her self-titled debut album in 1983; since then, she has revolutionized pop music by making her own persona a work of art. Her style and music have changed over the years, but they always remain bold and inventive. Her work is political, provocative, and unabashedly feminist, challenging people to think about women's bodies and power in a new way and championing freedom of expression without censorship. She is recognized as the bestselling female recording artist of all time, having sold more than 300 million records worldwide.

LIST YOUR ALL-TIME FAVORITE SONGS

What music is on your most-played list?

AUDRE LORDE'S *SISTER OUTSIDER*

Sister Outsider is a collection of essays and speeches by Audre Lorde (1934–1992), a self-described "black lesbian feminist warrior poet." Lorde writes about the complexities of an intersectional identity, drawing from her personal experiences with sexism, racism, homophobia, classism, and ageism. The conflict within the title reflects Lorde's idea that her intersectional identity as a black lesbian mother, poet, and partner in a racially mixed relationship provides her with a unique perspective as both a "sister" and an "outsider." For Lorde, it is exactly this complex identity that can be used to spark real change.

LIST YOUR IDENTIFIERS

**What communities and identities
do you align yourself with?**

_____

_____

_____

_____

_____

_____

_____

_____

LIST YOUR FIRSTS

What are the biggest first steps you've taken in your life?

_____

_____

_____

_____

_____

_____

_____

_____

_____

_____

WILMA MANKILLER: First Female Chief of the Cherokee Nation

In 1985, social worker Wilma Mankiller (1945–2010) became the first woman to be elected principal chief of the Cherokee Nation, a role she served for ten years. As principal chief, Mankiller doubled employment within the tribe, promoted better education, and revolutionized the healthcare system in the Cherokee Nation. She worked hard to promote Cherokee independence, improve the public image of Native Americans, and fight against the misappropriation of indigenous heritage. A tireless advocate for women's rights, Mankiller later returned to activism and authored numerous books. She was awarded the Presidential Medal of Freedom in 1998.

GUERRILLA GIRLS: Reinventing the "F" Word

Anonymous feminist activist artists known as the Guerrilla Girls are on a mission to fight against sexism in the art world. The group formed in reaction to the Museum of Modern Art's exhibit in 1985 that claimed to showcase "the era's most important painters and sculptors," where only 13 of the 165 artists were women. Wearing gorilla masks to keep the focus on the issues they address, the Guerrilla Girls make provocative public appearances such as museum takeovers and use humor and bold visuals to expose gender and ethnic inequality in the art world.

LIST YOUR FAVORITE ARTISTS

Who challenges your worldview?

_____

_____

_____

_____

_____

_____

_____

LIST YOUR POWER PIECES

What clothes do you wear to feel like your truest self?

_____

_____

_____

_____

_____

_____

_____

_____

_____

_____

JUDITH BUTLER'S *GENDER TROUBLE*

Gender Trouble: Feminism and the Subversion of Identity is one of the best-known works of superstar philosopher Judith Butler (b. 1956). Gender is not an innate personal attribute, Butler argues, but a social construct: People learn to perform in a certain way from their environment. According to Butler, conventional ideas about gender and sexuality serve to perpetuate patriarchal structures as well as to justify the oppression of queer people. Therefore, we need to completely shift our basic notions about gender, in order to make society better.

LIST YOUR RIDE OR DIES

Who's the Thelma to your Louise?

_____

_____

_____

_____

_____

_____

_____

THELMA & LOUISE

Thelma & Louise is a landmark film directed by Ridley Scott and written by Callie Khouri, who won an Oscar for her screenplay. Geena Davis stars as Thelma and Susan Sarandon as Louise, two friends who go on the run after killing the man who tried to rape Thelma. In the famous last scene, the women are cornered in their car by the police. Rather than spend their lives in jail, they kiss, step on the gas, and accelerate over a cliff and into the Grand Canyon. The film was a huge critical success and is regarded as an important piece of feminist cinema, showing empowered women taking action in the face of male aggression.

LIST YOUR BEST DIYS

What do you like making by hand?

_____

_____

_____

_____

_____

_____

_____

RIOT GRRRLS

In the early 1990s, all-female punk bands united to form the Riot Grrrl movement. Together, they confronted sexism in the music world by blending feminist consciousness with punk style and politics. The Riot Grrrls held regular meetings to discuss music as well as their experiences with sexism, body image, and identity. They organized to end homophobia, racism, sexism, and especially physical and emotional violence against women and girls. The Riot Grrrls also created zines and cassette tapes that they distributed widely as a way of saying "Screw you!" to commercial magazine and music publishers.

" . . . [Us] girls crave records and books and fanzines that speak to *us* that *we* feel included in and can understand in our own ways."

FIRST LINE OF THE
RIOT GRRRL MANIFESTO

LIST YOUR RAGES

What makes your blood boil?
What injustices do you stand up against?

_____

_____

_____

_____

_____

_____

_____

_____

ANITA HILL AND SEXUAL HARASSMENT AWARENESS

In 1991, Anita Hill (b. 1956) stood up against sexual harassment. Hill, an attorney and law professor, accused Supreme Court nominee Clarence Thomas, her boss at the Department of Education and the Equal Employment Opportunity Commission, of sexual harassment. Her brave and public testimony did not stop Thomas's confirmation, but it generated an awareness of what sexual harassment looks like in the workplace. The outcome mobilized women to political action, ultimately leading to the Violence Against Women Act, passed in 1994.

LIST YOUR FAVORITE PROTAGONISTS

Who are the women of literature who inspire you?

TONI MORRISON:
First African American Woman to Win the Nobel Prize in Literature

Toni Morrison (1931–2019) wrote her first novel, *The Bluest Eye* (1970), in fifteen-minute bursts each day before going to bed. It took her five years to finish the manuscript. In 1987, Morrison published her most celebrated novel, *Beloved*, for which she was awarded the Pulitzer Prize for Fiction. In 1993, Morrison was presented with the prestigious Nobel Prize in Literature—making her the first African American woman to receive this honor. In 2012, President Barack Obama presented Morrison with the Presidential Medal of Freedom to acknowledge her invaluable contribution to American literature.

LIST YOUR FANTASY DINNER PARTY GUESTS

Who do you want to chat up at a party?

_____

_____

_____

_____

_____

_____

_____

LIST YOUR MILLION-DOLLAR IDEAS

What will you be the boss of?

_____

_____

_____

_____

_____

_____

_____

LIST YOUR
FEMINIST CLASSICS

Which books would you put on your syllabus?

_____

_____

_____

_____

_____

_____

"Simply put,
feminism is a
movement to end
sexism, sexist
exploitation, and
oppression."

BELL HOOKS

FEMINISM IS FOR EVERYBODY: **By bell hooks**

Feminism Is for Everybody, by bell hooks (b. 1952), is a short, accessible introduction to feminist theory, meant to be read by all genders. A feminist classic, the book's aim is to rescue feminism from academic jargon, and more importantly, from its bad reputation. A professor and intersectional feminist thinker, hooks addresses the reader in a direct and sometimes provocative manner. She shows that the "F" word is not a dirty word, but rather a call for equal rights for everyone.

LIST YOUR NEWS RESOURCES

Where do you go to be informed?

_____

_____

_____

_____

_____

_____

_____

_____

_____

_____

FEMINISTING: Feminism Goes Online

Frustrated that the mainstream feminist discourse was excluding young feminists, journalist Jessica Valenti (b. 1978) and her sister Vanessa Valenti (b. 1980), set out to build a more accessible community and launched the site Feministing in 2004. The blog quickly became popular thanks to its bold, unapologetic tone and feminist analysis of everything from pop culture to politics. Columbia Journalism Review called Feministing "head and shoulders above almost any writing on women's issues in mainstream media."

LIST THE PEOPLE YOU LOVE

Who would you be lost without?

LOVE IS LOVE: Same-Sex Marriage

Same-sex marriage was finally legalized in all fifty states in 2015. In the Supreme Court case *Obergefell v. Hodges*, Ohio native Jim Obergefell sued his state for the permission to be listed as the surviving spouse on his terminally ill husband's death certificate. Justices ruled 5–4 that same-sex marriage is a constitutional right, guaranteed under the Fourteenth Amendment. As President Obama said about the case, "This ruling is a victory for America."

LIST YOUR LEADERSHIP QUALITIES

What does being a capable leader mean to you?

"Advancing the rights and opportunities
of women and girls is the great unfinished
business of the twenty-first century."

HILLARY CLINTON

HILLARY CLINTON:
First Female Presidential Nominee by a Major Political Party

Hillary Clinton (b. 1947) trained as a lawyer at Yale, was First Lady alongside President Bill Clinton from 1993 to 2001, and served as a Democratic senator from New York and as the secretary of state during President Barack Obama's administration (the first former First Lady to be elected to the US Senate and to hold a federal cabinet-level position). In the 2016 election, she became the first female candidate to be nominated for president by a major political party. Clinton founded Onward Together, a political organization dedicated to fund-raising for progressive political groups, and to building "a fairer, more inclusive America."

LIST YOUR BEST MARCHING CHANTS AND RALLY CRIES

What will you say to get people to listen?

WOMEN ARE PEOPLE

THE WOMEN'S MARCH

The Women's March on January 21, 2017, was a tour de force protest held in reaction to the inauguration of President Donald Trump the day prior. The largest march took place in Washington, DC, with sister marches in cities across the country and the world. It was the largest single-day protest in US history, and it was attended by an estimated five million people around the world. Protesters made a strong visual statement by wearing pink "pussyhats" as a representation of united female power and a positive appropriation of the word "pussy."

LIST YOUR SISTERS

Who do you look up to?
Who's making big changes in this world?

_____

_____

_____

_____

_____

THE "ME TOO" MOVEMENT

When #MeToo went viral in 2017, it ignited a long-overdue national conversation about sexual violence. Women finally felt they could speak up about their personal harassment stories, including ones involving prominent public figures. The phrase was originated in 2006 by activist Tarana Burke as a grassroots support network for survivors of sexual violence, particularly low-income women and women of color. "Me too" was a catchphrase for survivors to let others know they were not alone. The movement has since become a global network of women.

LIST YOUR LOFTIEST DREAMS

What do you want to be remembered for?

THE PINK WAVE

The 2018 midterms marked a sea change in Washington when a record 110 women (including another record-breaking forty-three women of color) were elected in an unprecedented "Pink Wave." The surge in female candidates can be attributed in part to the rising frustration among women regarding their rights, welfare, and safety, which also contributed to the founding of the #MeToo and Time's Up movements. Researchers have found that women are more likely to introduce legislation that helps other women and they sponsor more bills. And importantly, they serve as an inspiration for future generations of women to become politically engaged.

Editor: Madeline Jaffe
Designers: Diane Shaw and Melissa Faustine
Production Manager: Rebecca Westall

ISBN: 978-1-4197-4141-8

Printed and bound in China
10 9 8 7 6 5 4 3 2 1

Abrams Noterie products are available at special discounts when purchased
in quantity for premiums and promotions as well as fundraising or educational
use. Special editions can also be created to specification. For details, contact
specialsales@abramsbooks.com or the address below.

Abrams Noterie® is a registered trademark of Harry N. Abrams, Inc.

ABRAMS The Art of Books
195 Broadway, New York, NY 10007
abramsbooks.com

MIX
Paper from
responsible sources
FSC™ C144853